Amazing Trees

Written by Jill McDougall

🌱 Contents

What is a Tree?	2
Parts of a Tree	4
Trunks	6
Roots	10
Leaves	14
Picture Index	16

What is a Tree?

This book is about trees.

A tree is a kind of plant.
It has a woody stem called a trunk.

pine tree   apple tree   palm tree

woody stems

There are all kinds of trees.

Some trees are tiny. You can hold them in your hand.

Some trees are VERY BIG.

That's amazing!

Parts of a Tree

A tree has leaves, branches, a trunk and roots.

Each part has a job to do.

The leaves use the sun to make food for the tree.

The leaves grow from the branches.

Trunks

This is a redwood tree.
It is tall and its trunk is VERY BIG.

Redwood trees are the biggest trees on Earth.

A redwood tree can stay alive for 2000 years.

This tree is in North America.

A hole has been cut in the trunk of this redwood tree so that cars can go along the road.

7

This is a bottle tree.
Bottle trees grow where it is dry.

They hold water in their trunk, just like a bottle.

You can eat the leaves, seeds and roots of a bottle tree.

Roots

This is a pine tree.
It is growing on a dry hill.

It has long roots.

The roots have tiny hairs.
They soak up water for the tree.

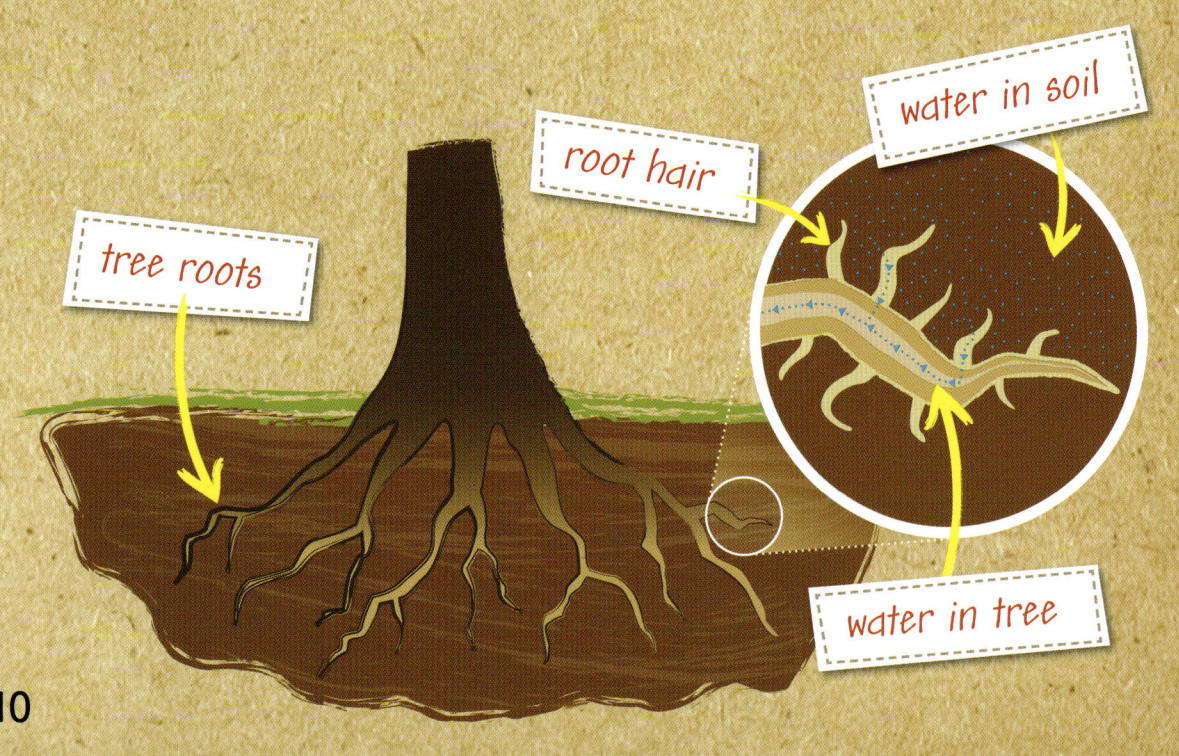

The roots grow into the soil to stop the tree falling over.

11

This is a mangrove tree.
Mangrove trees grow in salty water.

Salt is not good for trees.
These trees have long roots
to lift them up out of the water.

The roots make a
good home for fish.

The roots look like stilts!

Leaves

This is a cocoa tree.
Cocoa trees grow where it is wet.

Too much rain is not good for the trees.
The cocoa tree has shiny leaves
to help the rain slide off.

shiny leaves

The seeds of the cocoa tree are called cocoa beans. They are used to make chocolate ... yum!

I think trees are amazing!
Do you?

15

Picture Index

bottle tree   8–9

cocoa tree   14–15

mangrove tree   12–13

pine tree   10–11

redwood tree   6–7

16